Let's Rock!

EXPLORING
METAMORPHIC ROCKS

MARIE ROGERS

PowerKiDS
press

New York

Published in 2022 by The Rosen Publishing Group, Inc.
29 East 21st Street, New York, NY 10010

First Edition

Editor: Amanda Vink
Cover Designer: Alan Sliwinski
Interior Designer: Rachel Rising

Portions of this work were originally authored by Maria Nelson and published as *Metamorphic Rocks*. All new material in this edition authored by Marie Rogers.

Photo Credits: Cover, p. 17 Trygve Finkelsen/Shutterstock.com; Cover, pp. 1, 3, 4, 5, 6, 7, 8, 9, 10, 11, 12, 13, 15, 16, 18, 19, 20, 22, 23, 24 (background) Alex Konon/Shutterstock.com; p. 4 domnitsky/Shutterstock.com; p. 5 Bravo Ferreira da Luz/Shutterstock.com; p. 6 b-hide the scene/Shutterstock.com; pp. 7, 9 VectorMine/Shutterstock.com; p. 8 vvoe/Shutterstock.com; p. 11 Matauw/Shutterstock.com; p. 12 Stalev/Shutterstock.com; p.13 BlackRabbit3/Shutterstock.com; p. 14 Evgeny Haritonov/Shutterstock.com; p.15 Amit kg/Shutterstock.com; p.16 Breck P. Kent/Shutterstock.com; p. 18 Sakdinon Kadchiangsaen/Shutterstock.com; p 19 Tim Knight/Shutterstock.com; p. 20 MarcelClemens/Shutterstock.com; p. 21 Delli Maddalena/Shutterstock.com; p. 22 Madlen/Shutterstock.com.

Some of the images in this book illustrate individuals who are models. The depictions do not imply actual situations or events.

Library of Congress Cataloging-in-Publication Data

Names: Rogers, Marie, 1990- author.
Title: Exploring metamorphic rocks / Marie Rogers.
Description: New York : PowerKids Press, [2022] | Series: Let's rock! |
   Includes index.
Identifiers: LCCN 2019059512 | ISBN 9781725319219 (paperback) | ISBN
   9781725319233 (library binding) | ISBN 9781725319226 (6 pack)
Subjects: LCSH: Metamorphic rocks–Juvenile literature.
Classification: LCC QE475.A2 R64 2022 | DDC 552/.4-dc23
LC record available at https://lccn.loc.gov/2019059512

Manufactured in the United States of America

CPSIA Compliance Information: Batch #CWPK22. For further information contact Rosen Publishing, New York, New York at 1-800-237-9932.

Find us on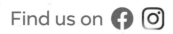

CONTENTS

CHANGEABLE

Rocks may appear permanent, or fixed, but they actually can change a lot over time. When the **environment** changes, rocks may move through stages of the rock cycle. Sometimes heat and forces are so great that a rock's **chemical** or **physical** makeup becomes altered. This creates metamorphic rocks.

The word "metamorphosis" has roots from the Greek language. It means "process of changing shape." Metamorphic rocks always begin as other rocks. Sometimes they start as igneous or sedimentary rocks, but they can also begin as one type of metamorphic rock and change to another. The original rock is called the protolith or the parent rock.

MARBLE ▶

ROCKING OUT

The rock cycle describes the different ways rocks can change over time. Rocks can form and break down depending on their environment. There are three types of rocks: metamorphic, igneous, and sedimentary.

Shown here is schist. It was first the sedimentary rock shale, but metamorphic forces changed it.

METAMORPHIC LOCATIONS

It takes high heat and force to make a metamorphic rock. Because of that, it's easiest to find metamorphic rocks in places that have **extreme** conditions. These places are often at the edges of the slow-moving plates of rock that make up Earth's surface. These are called tectonic plates. As tectonic plates shift, they can crash into one another. One plate may force another to go deeper underground or to lift up to face rain and other weather.

These major tectonic plates make up Earth's surface. The points where they meet are often places of extreme events such as volcanoes and earthquakes.

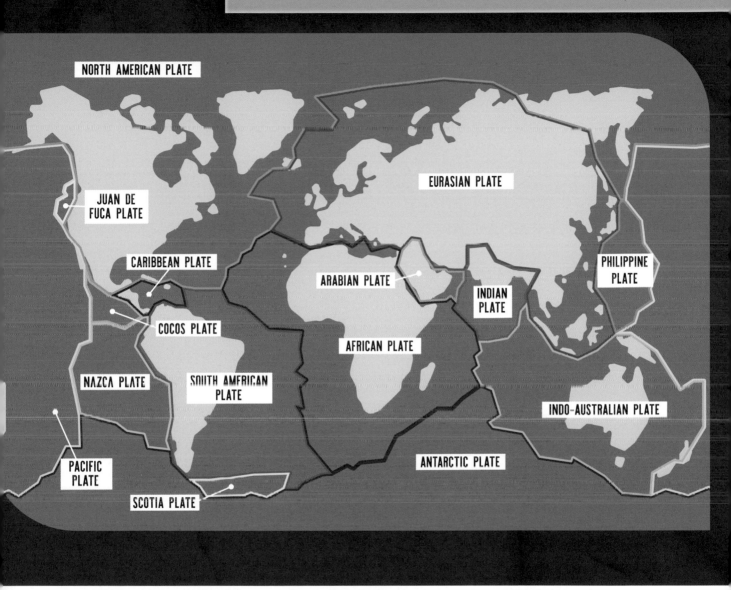

NORTH AMERICAN PLATE

JUAN DE FUCA PLATE

EURASIAN PLATE

CARIBBEAN PLATE

ARABIAN PLATE

PHILIPPINE PLATE

COCOS PLATE

INDIAN PLATE

AFRICAN PLATE

NAZCA PLATE

SOUTH AMERICAN PLATE

INDO-AUSTRALIAN PLATE

PACIFIC PLATE

ANTARCTIC PLATE

SCOTIA PLATE

Metamorphic rocks can also form in places with less extreme conditions. But because these changes happen more slowly and over a longer time, it's often harder to see them reflected in the finished rock.

WHAT CHANGES?

The lowest **temperature** that might cause metamorphic changes is about 300°Fahrenheit (149°Celsius). If the temperature gets too hot, the rock melts completely, and it's no longer a metamorphic rock.

Contact metamorphism can happen when magma, or melted rock under the ground, flows into or near solid rock. The very hot magma heats the cooler rock and bakes it. When this happens to a clay-rich rock, such as shale, the rock that forms is called hornfels. Farther away from the heat, the rock changes much less. If this happens in a small area, it's called local metamorphism.

HORNFELS ▷

If the temperature is too high, rock melts into magma.
When it cools and hardens, it becomes an igneous rock.

IGNEOUS ROCK

MAGMA

SEDIMENTARY ROCK

Melting

Heat and Pressure

METAMORPHIC ROCK

A rock can also become metamorphic when it's exposed to extreme force. This is called stress. The result is **strain** on the rock. Confining pressure is when the same force is used on all sides of the rock. In this case, the rock's **volume** is reduced. Directed stress may squash or stretch a rock by pressing on just one or two sides of it. In cases like these, the resulting rocks can look bent out of shape.

Regional metamorphism happens over a large area, such as when large continents move past one another. Rocks that form this way can often be found in the heart of mountain ranges.

Directed stress on this limestone in Crete, Greece, caused it to fold. The pressure came from more than one side.

ROCKING OUT

Sometimes chemical reactions can make metamorphic rocks. This can happen when different fluids, such as water or **dissolved** gases, meet one another and change one another.

MINERALS

Environmental conditions are only part of the story when it comes to forming metamorphic rocks. It also depends on what minerals are in the rock in the first place. Some minerals only melt at very high temperatures. Other minerals break easily. Often, when a rock's minerals break down during metamorphosis, the crystals will reform in a different way. Other times, the crystals won't grow back at all.

The minerals that form are more **stable** in the new environment. Sometimes the minerals separate by **density**. The rocks form in bands of color. Hornfels is a good example.

AMPHIBOLITE

12

ROCKING OUT

Minerals are the building blocks of rocks. Each mineral has its own special chemical makeup, which is always the same. In the right conditions, minerals grow crystals.

This picture of hornfels shows how the different minerals have created bands.

FOLIATION

When unequal pressure is applied to a metamorphic rock that has many minerals, sometimes the minerals position themselves in a way that's long and flat and **perpendicular** to the way the pressure was applied. These rocks have a striped look. They're called foliated metamorphic rocks. Some examples of often-foliated rocks are slate, phyllite, and gneiss.

Nonfoliated metamorphic rocks have one or just a few minerals in them. They're hard to see. Usually the stress on a nonfoliated metamorphic rock came from all directions. These types of metamorphic rocks can be **massive** or look grainy. Examples of often-nonfoliated metamorphic rocks are marble, quartzite, and soapstone.

NONFOLIATED ▶

ROCKING OUT

Humans have used soapstone for thousands of years. As early as the late Archaic period (3,000 to 5,000 years ago), Native Americans on the Pacific coast traveled about 60 miles (96.6 km) by canoe to get soapstone for making bowls and figurines.

Remember to look at texture, or how a rock feels, for foliation, not colors!

FOLIATED

CLASSIFICATION

Besides using a rock's texture and looks, scientists use a rock's chemical makeup to figure out what kind of metamorphic rock it is. Still, metamorphic rocks are commonly hard to **classify**. That's because there are so many things that can cause metamorphic changes. In addition, each rock reacts differently because of its chemical makeup.

Two common kinds of metamorphic rock—schist and gneiss—show just how hard metamorphic rock classification can be. Both can form from more than one kind of metamorphism and from more than one kind of rock. In fact, the rocks we call schist can come from igneous, sedimentary, or metamorphic rocks!

SCHIST

Scientists use systems to classify metamorphic rocks. They look at how a rock was affected by metamorphism, and then they look at the textures and minerals.

GNEISS

COMING TO YOU

Uplift brings metamorphic rock to Earth's surface. When tectonic plates crash into one another, it can create mountains and some land pushes up into the air. At the same time, other land masses can be buried. The exposed rock is subjected to weathering and erosion, processes in which rocks are slowly worn away over time by wind and weather.

The movement of tectonic plates is one way rocks move from place to place. In the new environments, rocks are forced to change. Scientists believe that if the processes of the rock cycle didn't happen—if rocks didn't change—Earth would be unable to support life.

SLATE ▶

ROCKING OUT

Impact metamorphism is another way metamorphic rocks form. That's when a volcano explodes suddenly or when a heavenly body such as a comet crashes into Earth.

This slate, a metamorphic rock, has been weathered and eroded by sand and wind.

HUMAN USES

Humans use metamorphic rocks for many things. People carved many famous statues out of marble, a metamorphic rock that forms when the sedimentary rock limestone is subjected to heat and pressure. People also often use metamorphic rocks as building materials, since they tend to be strong. Gneiss, for example, is often used for paving and as a building stone.

Lapis lazuli is also a metamorphic rock, although that might be surprising for many people! That's because of its bright blue color. It looks like a gemstone. People use it to make jewelry. The rock is made of multiple minerals. The blue color comes from the mineral lazurite.

LAPIS LAZULI ▶

The Italian artist Michelangelo carved this marble statue of David between 1501 and 1504.

PART OF OUR WORLD

Metamorphic rocks are an important part of our world. They're useful for humans. They also tell us a lot about the planet and how things change over time.

By studying these rocks' special bands and chemical makeup, scientists can tell us more about how Earth came to be as it is today. Metamorphic rocks especially tell scientists about conditions deep within Earth, such as the movement of tectonic plates.

What kind of metamorphic rocks are around you? See if you can find out where they came from!

GLOSSARY

chemical: Having to do with chemicals, or matter that can be mixed with other matter to cause changes.

classify: To group together by likeness.

density: The amount of matter something holds.

dissolve: To mix with a liquid and become part of the liquid.

environment: The conditions that surround a thing and affect it.

extreme: Very great in degree or severity.

massive: Very large, heavy, and solid.

perpendicular: Standing at a right angle to another surface or object.

physical: Existing in a form you can touch or see.

stable: In a condition that's not easily changed or likely to change.

strain: A force that pulls or stretches something.

temperature: How hot or cold something is.

volume: The amount of space taken up by a liquid, solid, or gas.

INDEX

WEBSITES

Due to the changing nature of Internet links, PowerKids Press has developed an online list of websites related to the subject of this book. This site is updated regularly. Please use this link to access the list:
www.powerkidslinks.com/letsrock/metamorphic